A Taste of Vietnam

Authentic, Homemade
Vietnamese Recipes
by Lan Truong

With many thanks...

To Danielle for your clear guidance, sensitive editing and for keeping things on track, and to James for translating my original design sympathetically and with patience. Finally, to my loving family for your unwavering support. x

First published in 2023 by Wrate's Publishing

ISBN 978-1-7393758-1-2

Copyright © Lan Truong, 2023

The right of Lan Truong to be identified as the author of this work has been asserted in accordance with the Copyright, Designs and Patents Act, 1988.

All rights reserved. No part of this publication may be reproduced, stored in a retrieval system, or transmitted, in any form or by any means (electronic, mechanical, photocopying, recording or otherwise), without the prior written permission of the publisher.

A CIP catalogue record for this book is available from the British Library.

Edited and typeset by
Wrate's Editing Services
www.wrateseditingservices.co.uk

Foreword

To celebrate the food of my home country, I have lovingly created this cookbook of homemade Vietnamese favourites. Using simple steps and great ingredients, I'll show you how to prepare delicious dishes that you can enjoy with your friends and family.

The advantage of living in the modern world is that you can visit your local shops and supermarkets and locate all the ingredients you'll need to experiment with different cuisines. In my experience, this applies to finding everything you will need to cook tasty and authentic Vietnamese dishes.

Having worked in catering and taught people how to cook Vietnamese food for several years, I have seen its popularity rise because of its freshness, its great taste and, of course, its healthiness!

So, let's get started. I hope you enjoy the experience!

Lan

Recipes

Sauces

12	**Dipping Fish Sauce**	
	Nước Mắm Chấm	
13	**Sweetened Fish Sauce**	
	Nước Mắm Pha	
13	**Salad Dressing**	
	Nước sốt xà lách	
14	**Blackened Caramelised Sauce**	
	Nước Màu	

Starters, Soups and Salads

16	**Fresh Salad Rolls**
	Gỏi cuốn
22	**Minced Prawns on Sugar Cane**
	Chạo Tôm
28	**Vietnamese Beef Steak Salad**
	Thịt bò bít tết
32	**Stir Fried Beef Noodle Salad**
	Bún thịt bò xào
36	**Vietnamese Fish Cakes**
	Chả cá
40	**Sizzling Beef Salad Rolls**
	Bò né
44	**Pomelo Salad**
	Gỏi Bưởi
48	**Carrot and White Radish Salad**
	Gỏi cà rốt và củ cải trắng
52	**Beef Noodle Soup**
	Phở Bò
56	**Chicken Noodle Soup**
	Phở Gà
60	**Sour Fish Soup**
	Canh chua cá
63	**Vietnamese Carrot and Cucumber Salad**
	Gỏi cà rốt và dưa leo
66	**Fried Spring Rolls**
	Chả giò

Main Courses

- 72 **Pan Fried Fish in Tomato Sauce**
  Cá chiên sốt cà
- 76 **Stuffed Tofu in Tomato Sauce**
  Đậu hũ nhồi thịt xốt cà chua
- 80 **La Vong Fish Cakes**
  Chả cá Lã Vọng
- 84 **Chicken with Lemongrass and Chilli**
  Gà xào sả ớt
- 88 **Stir Fried Mixed Vegetables with Beef**
  Rau thập cẩm xào với thịt bò
- 92 **Tender Rolled Beef in Chinese Five Spice**
  Bò hầm cuốn Ngũ vị
- 96 **Braised Fish**
  Cá kho
- 100 **Southern Crispy Crepes**
  Bánh xèo Nam Bộ
- 104 **Chicken with Ginger**
  Gà kho gừng
- 107 **Stir Fried Beans with Prawns**
  Đậu que xào với Tôm
- 110 **Prawns with Garlic and Chillies**
  Tôm rang với tỏi và ớt

Desserts

- 114 **Banana Fritters With Ice Cream**
  Chuối chiên với kem
- 118 **Banana Cake**
  Bánh Chuối nướng
- 122 **Pineapple Tartlets**
  Bánh Tạc nhân thơm
- 128 **Tapioca Cake**
  Bánh khoai mì

Basic Ingredients

These ingredients are used daily in Vietnam. You might not be familiar with all of them, but I have tried my best to use ingredients that you can easily find in the supermarket or your local Asian store.

Aravi: a member of the taro family, this is a very versatile and popular ingredient. It is used in savoury dishes and in desserts. These are mostly available in Asian stores.

Boston or butter lettuce: known for its sweet flavour and tender texture, the leaves are flexible and good for wrapping.

Chicken stock cubes: used to enhance the flavour of a dish.

Chinese five spice: a combination of star anise, fennel seeds, cinnamon, cloves and Szechuan peppercorns. Ground well, it is a strong, aromatic seasoning. Only a small amount is required.

Coriander: also known as cilantro or Chinese parsley, its leaves are used as a garnish.

Dill: a herb in the celery family, it is widely used in Vietnamese cooking.

Fish sauce: made from fermented fish and salt, this is used daily in Vietnamese cooking, either as a marinade or diluted with sugar and lime juice to make a dipping sauce.

Fresh coconut juice: used widely in Vietnam as a hydrating drink or in cooking to add natural sweetness to a dish. You can find it in cans in most supermarkets, and this can be used as a substitute for its fresh equivalent.

Galangal: related to ginger, it has a stronger flavour. When used in marinating, the skin must be peeled off and the flesh mashed well.

Glass noodles: these are translucent and made from mung bean starch. They are usually included in spring rolls to add texture.

Hoisin sauce: a thick, dark, concentrated sauce. It is very sweet and mainly used in Chinese cuisine. A small amount is added to a bowl of noodle soup to elevate the flavour. It is also used when making dipping sauce.

Hot chilli sauce (Sriracha brand): made from a paste of chilli peppers, it is used as a dipping sauce. Alternatively, a small amount can be added to a bowl of noodle soup to give a tangy taste.

Knorr or Maggi seasoning: a dark brown liquid with a mild flavour. A small amount can be used to marinate meat, fish and poultry.

Lemongrass: an intensely fragrant herb that is popular in Vietnamese cooking. Only the thick part of the stem near the root is edible. It can be found in most supermarkets.

Lime: a green citrus fruit. It has a sharp, acidic taste.

Mint: known worldwide for its fresh flavour, it can be used as a garnish, to make drinks or added to salads.

Oyster sauce: made from oyster extract, sugar, salt and water thickened with corn starch, various brands are available in most supermarkets.

Pak choi: Also known as bok choy, it is a leafy, green type of Chinese cabbage. Its leaves are broad, tapering to white stalks that are crisp and crunchy.

Pomelo: popular in Southeast Asia, it is like grapefruit, but the texture is firmer, and the taste sweeter. It's great for using in salads.

Red Thai chillies: also known as bird's eye chillies, they are extremely hot.

Rice flour: made from finely milled rice. Different types of rice flour are available in supermarkets, but for southern crepes, I find the rice flour from Thailand produces the best texture.

Rice noodles: a daily staple in Vietnam. They can be used in noodle soups, salads and fresh rolls. Available in Asian stores.

Rice paper: made from rice flour, water and salt; it is steamed and dried in the sun on bamboo racks. Rice paper is widely used in Vietnam for a variety of rolls.

Rice sticks: these wide, medium-thick noodles are used in noodle soup (Pho) and are very popular in Vietnam.

Rice vermicelli: a thin form of rice noodles, they are usually used in stir fries or noodle salads.

Shallots: also called baby onions, these are used daily in Vietnamese cooking. They are commonly fried in oil to give dishes a pleasant aroma.

Star anise: has a strong, pungent fragrance. It is usually combined with other spices to add flavour to a dish.

Sugar cane: found in hot, tropical countries, it is used to make sugar and drinks. In Vietnam, we often use it in food, utilising its natural sweetness.

Tapioca starch: made from cassava root, when prepared properly, it provides a distinctive taste and is mostly used in desserts.

Tamarind juice: used in most cuisines as a souring agent, cooking tamarind is available in most supermarkets in the form of a compressed block. To obtain tamarind juice, cut a small piece from the block and soak it in boiled water for five minutes before mashing well and straining.

Tofu or bean curd: made from soybean, it is a very healthy vegetarian food. In Southeast Asian cuisine, it is cooked in different forms.

White radish: also known as daikon, it resembles a large white carrot and is used widely in Vietnamese cooking for making stock for soups.

Wood ear mushrooms: these have little flavour, but they are normally used to add crunch to a dish.

Measurements

All the recipes in this book are based on the following measurements:

1 teaspoon (tsp) = 5ml
1 tablespoon (tbsp) = 15ml
1 cup = 250ml (roughly 8oz)
500ml = 1 pint

Lengths

12mm = ½ inch
2.5cm = 1 inch

Weights

250g = 9oz
500g = 1.1lb

Oven temperature

	°C	°F
Low	150	300
Moderate	180	350
Medium	200	400
Hot	220	425
Very Hot	230	450

Sauces

A Vietnamese meal isn't complete without a sauce or dressing. We often complement our food with a tasty shrimp or fish paste, but these are quite pungent and too strong for a lot of people. More commonly, we use one of the more popular sauces listed in this section, which will certainly elevate the flavour of your chosen recipe.

Dipping Fish Sauce
Nước Mắm Chấm

Sweetened Fish Sauce
Nước Mắm Pha

Salad Dressing
Nước sốt xà lách

Blackened Caramelised Sauce
Nước Màu

Dipping Fish Sauce
Nước Mắm Chấm

If you are invited by a Vietnamese family for a meal, it's highly likely you'll see a small bowl of fish sauce on the side.

Depending on the dish and individual preference, fish sauce can be left salty and served straight out of the bottle, with the addition of some chopped chillies and a squeeze of lime juice. At other times, a small amount of sugar can be added to the sauce to sweeten it and lighten up the dish.

Ingredients

- 4 tbsp sugar
- 400ml boiling water
- 6 tbsp fish sauce
- 2 garlic cloves (crushed)
- 2 chopped chillies
- 3 tbsp lime juice

Method

1. Mix the sugar with the boiling water in a large bowl.
2. Stir well and leave until the sugar dissolves in the water and everything has cooled down.
3. Add fish sauce to the mixture to your taste.
4. Add garlic, chillies and lime juice and taste again.

Sweetened Fish Sauce
Nước Mắm Pha

This is similar to the Dipping Fish Sauce, but it is slightly saltier, as you'll mix it with noodles.

Ingredients

- 4 tbsp sugar
- 400ml boiling water
- 10 tbsp fish sauce
- 2 garlic cloves (crushed)
- 2 chopped chillies
- 3 tbsp lime juice

Method

1. In a large bowl, mix the sugar with the boiling water.
2. Stir well and leave until the sugar dissolves in the water and everything cools down.
3. Add the fish sauce to the mixture, to your taste.
4. Add the garlic, chillies and lime juice, and taste again.

Salad Dressing
Nước sốt xà lách

For salads, we generally use a very light dressing that is simple to make and adds freshness and balance to the dish.

Ingredients

- 2 tbsp sugar
- 200ml boiling water
- 4 tbsp fish sauce
- 1 garlic clove (crushed)
- 1 chopped chilli
- 3 tbsp lime juice

Method

1. In a bowl, mix the sugar with the boiling water.
2. Stir well and leave until the sugar dissolves in the water and everything cools down.
3. Add the fish sauce, garlic, chilli and lime juice, and stir well.

Blackened Caramelised Sauce
Nước Màu

This is an essential sauce for braising, as it gives dishes colour and depth of flavour. It is made using brown sugar and, when making it, you need to pay 100% attention to the task in hand, as it can so easily burn. When the sauce cools down, place it in a jar and store it in the fridge, where it can last for up to a year.

Ingredients

- 2 cups brown sugar
- 1 cup water

Method

1. Heat the brown sugar in a non-stick, medium-size saucepan until it starts to liquefy. Turn the heat to low.
2. Stir occasionally so that the sugar doesn't stick to the bottom of the pan.
3. When the sugar starts to turn black, stir continuously.
4. Continue to stir until the sugar turns completely black.
5. Remove from the heat and leave to cool for 3 minutes.
6. Put back on the heat (still low heat) and add water. Stir continuously until the sugar has dissolved in the water.
7. Bring to the boil. Then turn the heat to low. Simmer for 15 minutes, stirring occasionally, until the liquid slightly thickens.

Starters, Soups and Salads

Fresh Salad Rolls
Gỏi cuốn

Minced Prawns on Sugar Cane
Chạo Tôm

Vietnamese Beef Steak Salad
Thịt bò bít tết

Stir Fried Beef Noodle Salad
Bún thịt bò xào

Vietnamese Fish Cakes
Chả cá

Sizzling Beef Salad Rolls
Bò né

Pomelo Salad
Gỏi Bưởi

Carrot and White Radish Salad
Gỏi cà rốt và củ cải trắng

Beef Noodle Soup
Phở Bò

Chicken Noodle Soup
Phở Gà

Sour Fish Soup
Canh chua cá

Vietnamese Carrot and Cucumber Salad
Gỏi cà rốt và dưa leo

Fried Spring Rolls
Chả giò

Fresh Salad Rolls
Gỏi cuốn

Fresh Salad Rolls are the ultimate healthy Vietnamese street food. Go to any market or food court and you will find a stall selling them. The rolls are folded beautifully by skilful hands and are displayed in glass cabinets. The fresh pink prawns and vivid green herbs are eye-catching.

The advantage of these rolls is that you don't have to stick to the ingredients listed here. As long as you choose ingredients that complement each other, you can add anything that takes your fancy, and even leftovers. This is my version, which is a good one to start with. So, let's rock and roll.

Ingredients (serves 6)

- 300g chicken breast (skin and bones removed)
- 150ml coconut juice
- 500g medium tiger prawns
- A pinch of salt
- 100g rice vermicelli
- 300g cucumber
- 200g lettuce
- 100g mint
- 100g coriander
- 100g sweet basil (optional)
- 200g bean sprouts
- 12-15 pieces of rice paper (22cm)
- Water as specified in each stage

Cooking the chicken

1. Rinse the chicken fillet.
2. In a saucepan, bring to a boil 100ml of water, 100ml of coconut juice from the can and a pinch of salt.
3. Add the chicken breast, removing any froth that appears on the surface of the water. When there is no more froth, reduce to a medium heat.
4. If necessary, add some more water, leaving the chicken to cook for 20 minutes, turning it occasionally.
5. Remove the chicken from the stock, set it aside and leave it to cool. Keep the chicken stock for use later in the dipping sauce.

Cooking the prawns

1. Remove the heads and devein the prawns but retain the shells. Rinse the prawns well.
2. In a saucepan, bring to a boil 50ml of water, 50ml coconut juice and a pinch of salt.
3. Add the prawns and cook them for 4 minutes on each side.
4. Drain the prawns and set them aside.
5. Keep the prawn stock for use later in the dipping sauce.

Preparing the fillings

1. Boil the rice vermicelli in a saucepan containing 1ltr water. Cook for 3 minutes. Taste and when cooked, rinse with cold water. Leave until all the excess water has drained off.
2. Wash the vegetables and herbs thoroughly and leave them to dry. When cutting the cucumbers, retain the skin. Cut off both ends, cut them in half along the length and slice them diagonally.
3. Slice the chicken thinly, and remove the shells from the prawns, cutting them in half along their length.

Rolling the rolls

1. Moisten both sides of a piece of rice paper with water and place on a flat surface.
2. Break the lettuce into small pieces and place them on top of the rice paper, close to the edge nearest to you.
3. Add the mint, coriander, sweet basil (optional), bean sprouts, sliced cucumber, rice vermicelli and the sliced chicken.
4. Fold over, then fold in the sides and roll, adding two pieces of prawn to complete the parcel.

Dipping Sauce

Ingredients

- 2 tbsp vegetable oil
- 5 shallots (chopped)
- 2 garlic cloves (crushed)
- 100ml Hoisin sauce
- 50ml chicken stock (as previously prepared)
- 50ml prawn stock (as previously prepared)
- 150ml coconut milk
- 1 tsp smooth peanut butter
- 20ml water
- A few drops of oyster and fish sauce (optional)

Method

1. In the vegetable oil, sauté the shallots and garlic over a medium heat until golden brown.
2. Add the Hoisin sauce, chicken and prawn stocks, coconut milk, peanut butter, water and, if required, the fish and/or oyster sauce.
3. Bring to the boil, season to taste and simmer for 30 minutes.

Useful tip: You can make a large amount of the dipping sauce, divide it into small portions and freeze it for later use.

Minced Prawns on Sugar Cane
Chạo Tôm

For those hailing from tropical countries, sugar cane, which is a type of grass, is used to make a refreshing juice that is perfect for rehydrating during hot and humid weather. I still remember when I was young, cycling along a road in Saigon under a scorching sun, my throat dry, looking for something to drink. Suddenly, I saw a sugar cane machine on the pavement. A man was using all his strength to turn the wheel of the machine to squeeze the juice out of the sugar cane sticks and kumquats. I stopped my bike beside him and ordered a glass of juice, taking a long gulp of the cold, sweet and slightly sour liquid. I can't describe how great I felt.

Another way we use sugar cane is in food, as my recipe will reveal...

I have always adored this dish. Whenever I am back in Vietnam and go to a restaurant, I just have to order it. It is usually served on a winnowing basket, and everything is displayed so nicely. You can see the fresh herbs, rice paper, noodles and, of course, the minced prawns on the sugar cane. You then take a piece of rice paper, place a bit of everything inside it, roll it up and dip one end in the dipping sauce. When you take a bite, the combination of the fresh herbs and the minced prawns, which are slightly sweet after being grilled with the sugar cane, is delicious. The aroma is also unforgettable.

Enough reminiscing... I think it's time to share my recipe with you.

Ingredients (serves 6)

- 700g medium tiger prawns
- 300g chicken thighs (skin, bone removed)
- 2 spring onions
- 3 garlic cloves
- 6 shallots
- ⅓ tsp salt
- 1 tsp corn flour
- ⅓ tsp sugar
- ½ tsp ground black pepper
- 2 tsp oyster sauce
- 2 sugar cane sticks
- Vegetable oil
- 200g dry rice vermicelli
- 20 pieces rice paper (22cm)
- 200g lettuce
- 100g mint
- 100g coriander
- 300g cucumber (sliced)

Preparing the ingredients

1. Devein and fully clean the prawns and then give them and the chicken thighs a good rinse. Using a colander, drain all the excess water from the prawns and chicken.
2. Chop the spring onion, garlic and shallots in a blender, transfer them to a bowl and set aside. Cut the chicken thighs into small pieces then mince well in a blender. Add the prawns and mince again until a mousse is formed.
3. Place the mousse in a bowl, add the chopped spring onions, shallots, garlic, salt, corn flour, sugar, ground black pepper and oyster sauce. Mix well and then, using a fork, fold for 5 minutes. Leave to marinate for an hour in the fridge.

Cutting the sugar cane

1. Using a cleaver, remove the skin of the sugar cane.
2. Cut the cane into small pieces of around 12cm in length. Then cut into 4 pieces along the length.

Making the prawn on sugar cane

1. Moisten the palm of your hand and the pieces of sugar cane with oil.
2. Take a small amount of the prawn mixture and spread it around the sugar cane in a thin layer, about half a centimetre thick, to form an oval ball shape.

Cooking the prawn on sugar cane

1. Use either charcoal to grill the prawn on sugar cane or an oven grill set to a medium-high heat.
2. Thinly coat an oven tray with vegetable oil. Lay out the prawn on sugar cane in even rows and grill, rotating until all the sides are golden brown.
3. Boil the rice vermicelli for 3 minutes, taste and, when cooked, rinse with cold water and then leave for the excess water to drain. Wash all the vegetables well.

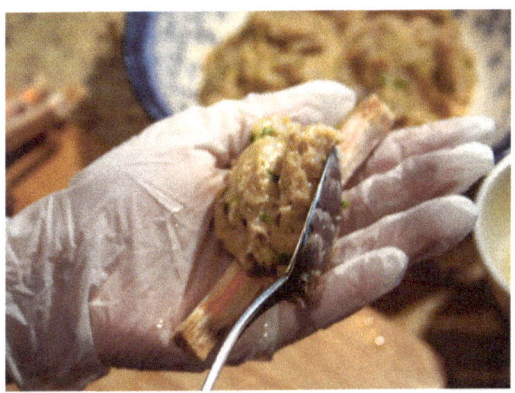

To serve

Halve the minced prawns along their length to remove the minced prawn from the sugar cane, which you can now discard. Moisten the rice paper with water and put the lettuce, mint, coriander, cucumber, rice vermicelli and the grilled, minced prawn inside it. Fold it up and dip it into the dipping sauce.

Making the dipping sauce

See page 20.

> **Useful tip:** You can partially grill the prawn on sugar cane in advance, grilling again just before serving.

Vietnamese Beef Steak Salad
Thịt bò bít tết

With the hardship of earning a living in Vietnam, my mum couldn't afford to buy each of us 3 kids a piece of steak. Instead, she used to buy a single piece, probably not the best cut either, which she sliced thinly and used to make this tasty dish, which we shared as a family. I still vividly remember the smell of the garlic and the steak, as my mum fried them together.

This dish is quick and easy to prepare, and it provides real comfort food.

You don't have to use Boston lettuce; you can use any kind of lettuce available. Just slice the lettuce leaves and place them evenly on a plate, and then pile up the other ingredients on top.

Ingredients (serves 4)

- 300g rump steak (or any cut available)
- ¼ tsp salt
- ¼ tsp ground black pepper
- ½ tsp Knorr seasoning
- 1 tsp oyster sauce
- 2 garlic cloves (crushed)
- A pinch of sugar
- 300g Boston lettuce (or any type of lettuce)
- 2 tomatoes (thinly sliced)
- Vegetable oil
- 2 small potatoes (peeled and thinly sliced)
- 1 onion (cut into wedges)

Dressing

- 1 tsp lemon juice
- Chopped chillies (optional)
- 2 tsp sugar
- 50ml water
- 2 tbsp Knorr seasoning
- 1 tsp lemon juice
- Chopped chillies (optional)

Preparing the beef

1. Rinse the beef under the tap, then drain the water from the meat using a colander.
2. Use a sharp knife to remove all the fat and veins from the beef and thinly slice it.
3. Add salt, black pepper, Knorr seasoning, oyster sauce, crushed garlic and a pinch of sugar.
4. Mix well and leave to marinate for an hour in the fridge.

Preparing the salad

1. If you are using Boston lettuce, separate the lettuce leaves. If you are using other types of lettuce, slice the leaves and arrange them evenly on a large plate.
2. Thinly slice the tomatoes and sprinkle a little sugar over them. Arrange them on top of the lettuce.

Cooking the beef

1. Heat 100ml of oil in a frying pan over a high heat. When hot, fry the thinly cut potato slices.
2. When each potato slice is golden brown, remove from the oil and place on top of the tomatoes.
3. Using the same frying pan, remove some of the oil and add the onion wedges.
4. Stir quickly and then add the beef, stirring for approximately 3 minutes.
5. When the beef is slightly brown, remove it from the pan together with the onions and arrange them on top of the potatoes.

Making the dressing

1. In a small bowl, mix 2 teaspoons of sugar with 50ml of boiling water.
2. Let the water cool down and add the 2 tablespoons of Knorr seasoning, 1 teaspoon of lemon juice and some chopped chillies (optional).
3. Mix well and taste.

To serve

Take one of the filled lettuce leaves, or scoop the sliced lettuce leaves with all the topping, drizzle some dressing on the top and enjoy.

> **Useful tip:** You can use any other type of lettuce, but the best types are those where the leaf forms the shape of a cup.

Stir Fried Beef Noodle Salad
Bún thịt bò xào

My mum used to cook this dish for us kids when we had grown bored with rice and everyday dishes. It was, and still is, a real treat. I loved the taste of all the fresh herbs, such as the sweet basil, Korean perilla (or shisho) and Vietnamese balm, and the chopped cucumber and bean sprouts mixed with the succulent beef, noodles, chopped nuts and sweetened fish sauce, which made the taste so addictive.

I often had an extra bowl, because one serving didn't seem enough. Since living away from home, I have cooked this dish from time to time, and it's still one of the easiest and freshest recipes I have ever come across. So, if you fancy trying something new, give this salad a go.

Ingredients (serves 6)

- 700g rump steak (or any cut available)
- ⅓ tsp salt
- ⅓ tsp sugar
- ⅓ tsp ground black pepper
- 1 tsp Knorr seasoning
- 2 tsp oyster sauce
- 3 garlic cloves (finely chopped)
- 300g lettuce
- 200g mint
- 200g coriander
- 3 small cucumbers
- 300g bean sprouts
- 400g dry rice noodles or vermicelli
- Vegetable oil
- 100g spring onions (chopped)
- 100g roasted peanuts (crushed)
- 2 onions (cut into wedges)

Preparing the beef

1. Rinse the steak under a tap, then drain the water from the meat using a colander.
2. Use a sharp knife to remove all the fat and veins from the beef and thinly slice it.
3. Place it in a bowl with the salt, sugar, ground black pepper, Knorr seasoning, oyster sauce and chopped garlic.
4. Mix well and leave to marinate for 2 hours.

Preparing the salad

1. Wash the lettuce, mint and coriander and drain the excess water using a colander.
2. Once dry, finely chop your bunch of herbs and lettuce.
3. Wash the cucumber, cut off the ends and cut it into small strips.
4. Wash the bean sprouts.

Cooking the noodles

1. Fill a large saucepan with water, bring it to the boil and add the rice noodles, stirring to separate them.
2. Turn the heat down. Put the lid on the pan but leave a small gap. If you are using rice noodles, cook for 20 minutes (stirring occasionally); rice vermicelli will cook in around 3 minutes.
3. When cooked to your taste, rinse with cold water and drain well in a colander for 1 hour before serving.

Spring onions

1. In a small frying pan, heat 50ml of oil.
2. Add the chopped spring onion and fry for 1 minute, then remove from the heat. Set aside. Crush the roasted nuts.

Cooking the beef

1. Heat 100ml of oil in a large frying pan. Once hot, add the onion wedges. Stir and add the beef.
2. Continue to stir for about 4 minutes until the meat has browned slightly. Remove it from the heat.

Putting it together

1. For each guest, place in a bowl a layer of the chopped lettuce, mint, coriander, bean sprouts, cucumber, noodles, beef, fried spring onion and nuts.
2. Before serving your salad, drizzle some sweetened fish sauce over the top.

Making the sweetened fish sauce

See page 13.

> **Useful tip:** For tender meat, always slice across the grain.

Vietnamese Fish Cakes
Chả cá

These fish cakes are loved by Vietnamese people for their bouncy and elastic texture. They're one of my favourite 'street food' snacks that I make when I'm away from home. When I'm craving something savoury, they often spring to mind. And when you're hungry for something in particular, you have to find a way to get it – or make it yourself! I find kingfish is the ideal fish to use, and it's available from most supermarkets.

The advantage of kingfish is that it's meaty and easy to separate from the bones. Back in Vietnam, I used to beat and fold the flesh of the fish by hand to create the body for the cakes, but this took ages. Nowadays, I use an electric blender to help in cutting and blending the flesh together. A method that's less work and creates more taste is definitely the one to go with!

Ingredients (serves 4)

- 3 spring onions
- 1-2 small red Thai chillies
- 6 shallots
- 50g dill
- 750g king fish
- ⅓ tsp salt
- ½ tsp sugar
- 2 tsp oyster sauce
- 2 tsp fish sauce
- 1 tsp corn flour
- ⅓ tsp baking powder
- ½ tsp ground black pepper
- Vegetable oil

Preparing the vegetables

1. Wash the spring onions, chillies and shallots.
2. Drain the water from them using a colander.
3. Once dry, roughly cut them into small pieces before transferring them to a blender to finely chop. Remove and set aside.
4. Wash the dill and drain the water using a colander. Roughly cut the dill into small pieces (do not blend) and set aside.

Preparing the fish

1. Wash the kingfish pieces and drain the water using a colander.
2. Separate the flesh from the skin.
3. Discard the skin, bones and blood lines.
4. Put the flesh in the blender.
5. Blend well until you have the texture of a mousse.

Making the paste

1. Add the chopped shallots, chillies, spring onions, dill, salt, sugar, oyster sauce, fish sauce, corn flour, baking powder and ground black pepper to the blender and blend thoroughly. Beat and fold with a fork.
2. Leave to chill in the fridge for 2 hours.

Forming the cakes

1. Take a 21cm diameter flat plate and coat the surface and a tablespoon with oil.
2. Take a spoonful of fish mousse, place it on the plate and use the spoon to flatten it to form a roughly circular fish cake shape, approximately 0.5 cm thick.

Useful tip: You can choose any white fish, as long as it has a fine texture and a shiny, slightly slippery surface. This is what will give the fishcakes body.

Cooking the cakes

1. Fill a deep, 22cm diameter non-stick frying pan to about a third of its depth with oil.
2. Place it over a high heat. When the oil is hot, use a tablespoon to gently slide the fish cake from the plate into the liquid.
3. Turn the heat down to medium, so the fish cake cooks throughout.
4. When one side is golden brown, gently flip the cake over.
5. Cook until both sides are golden brown.
6. Remove from the frying pan and drain the excess oil using a sieve.
7. Repeat these steps until all the fish cake mixture has been used up.
8. Serve with either hot or sweet chilli sauce.

Sizzling Beef Salad Rolls
Bò né

This dish is normally served in open-air restaurants. As we cheekily joke, "There are Michelin Star restaurants in the West, but there are multi-star restaurants in Vietnam." Growing up, I visited them on a regular basis – indoor restaurants with air conditioning were too extravagant – and the food in outdoor restaurants was always good. We often cooked our own food at the table and shared it out amongst us, so it was a very casual and fun affair. You always came home with the smell of the food in your hair and clothes, while feeling full and satisfied.

This dish is fun to share with friends and family. The good thing is, you can help get all the ingredients prepared and then set everything out on the table. If the weather outside is gorgeous and sunny, why not set a table up in the garden and take it in turns to cook the beef and make the rolls, chatting while you do so? Go on, give it a try – I bet the smell of the food will make the neighbours jealous!

Ingredients (serves 4)

- 5 sticks of lemongrass
- 6 shallots
- 4 garlic cloves
- 1kg rump steak or any cuts available
- ⅓ tsp salt
- 2 tsp oyster sauce
- ½ tsp Knorr seasoning
- 2 tsp ground Chinese five spice
- ⅔ tsp ground black pepper
- ½ tsp sugar
- 200g rice vermicelli
- 3 small cucumbers
- 1 large, ripe pineapple
- 400g lettuce
- 200g mint
- 200g coriander
- 30 pieces of rice paper
- A small jug of vegetable oil

Equipment required

- Portable gas stove and a small frying pan.

Preparing the vegetables

1. Take the lemongrass sticks and remove the dry root ends and the dry outer leaf, retaining only the thick part of the herb. Chop each stick into 0.5cm long pieces.
2. In a blender, grind the lemongrass, shallots and garlic.

Preparing the beef

1. Rinse the steak under a tap, then drain the water from the meat using a colander.
2. Use a sharp knife to remove all the fat and veins from the beef and thinly slice it.
3. Place it in a bowl with the ground lemongrass mixture, salt, oyster sauce, Knorr seasoning, Chinese five spice, ground black pepper and sugar.
4. Mix thoroughly and leave to marinate for an hour.

Preparing the fillings

1. Boil the rice vermicelli for 3 minutes, taste and, when cooked, rinse with cold water. Leave to drain.
2. Wash all the vegetables thoroughly and leave them to dry. Retaining the skin of the cucumbers, cut off the ends, then cut them in half along the length and diagonally slice them. Remove the skin and core of the pineapple. Thinly slice.

Setting the table

1. Prepare two bowls of water for moistening the rice paper and a small bowl for each guest containing the dipping fish sauce.
2. Arrange the lettuce, mint and coriander on a large plate and prepare separate plates containing the rice vermicelli, sliced cucumber, pineapple and rice paper.

Making the dipping fish sauce

See page 12.

To serve

1. Turn on the gas stove. When the frying pan is really hot, drizzle some oil into it. Add a small amount of beef and stir fry quickly for 1 minute. Remove the beef from the frying pan.
2. Moisten both sides of a piece of rice paper with water. Break the lettuce into small pieces and place on top of it, close to the edge nearest to you. Add the mint, coriander, vermicelli noodles, pineapple, cucumber and, finally, put the beef on top. Fold over, roll and dip into the fish sauce. Enjoy!

> **Useful Tip:** To save time you can prepare the beef the day before and leave it to marinate in the fridge overnight.

Pomelo Salad
Gỏi Bưởi

Pomelo is a tropical citrus fruit that is very popular in South East Asia. It's like grapefruit, but it tastes sweeter and has a firmer texture. It is widely used in Vietnam, where it is believed the citrus is good for cleansing and detoxing the body. I was told that if you eat a small amount of pomelo for breakfast every day, it'll help you to lose weight in a healthy way.

In Vietnam, we use the skin of the pomelo for making sweet desserts. In the olden days, we also used to dry the skins in the sun, boil them and then mix them with cold water to use for washing our hair. It was a good way to keep our tresses shiny and to prevent hair loss.

Much like the carrot and cucumber salad, making Pomelo Salad is not a quick job, but it's well worth it. It's one of the freshest and healthiest meals you'll ever taste.

Ingredients (serves 6)

- 1 pomelo
- 100ml white vinegar
- 1 tsp sugar
- 2 carrots
- 1 large onion
- 500g medium tiger prawns
- 100ml coconut juice
- Pinch of salt
- 50g mint (roughly chopped)
- 50g coriander (roughly chopped)
- 50g shallots (chopped)
- 50ml vegetable oil
- 30g roast peanuts (crushed)

Removing the skin of the pomelo

1. First, cut off the 'pointy' end. Now cut deep lines along the length of the fruit and peel the skin.
2. Cut the pomelo into segments and gently remove the flesh peeling off the membrane. Break into small pieces and arrange evenly on a large, deep plate (3-5cm deep).

Making the pickle

1. In a small saucepan, mix the white vinegar with the sugar and 50ml of water. Bring to the boil and set aside to cool.
2. Using a potato peeler or mandolin, thinly slice the carrots and onion and place them in a bowl. Pour the vinegar mixture over them, mix well and then leave to marinate for 2 hours, stirring occasionally.

Preparing the prawns

1. Remove the heads and devein the prawns, retaining the shells. Rinse well.
2. To a small saucepan, add the coconut juice, a pinch of salt and 50ml of water. Bring to the boil, add the prawns and cook well.
3. Drain the prawns using a colander. When they have cooled down, remove the shells and halve them along their length.

Putting the salad together

1. Place the pomelo flesh on a large, deep plate. Take a clean tea towel, put the carrots and onion mixture inside it and squeeze to remove the liquid. Then, place a layer of it on top of the pomelo.
2. Sprinkle the mint and coriander over the carrots and onion, and then arrange the prawns on top.
3. Sauté the shallots in 50ml of oil until lightly browned. Remove from the heat and keep stirring until they are evenly coloured. Set aside to cool down.
4. Pour the fried shallots on top of the prawns.

To serve

Sprinkle the dish with the crushed roasted nuts and salad dressing.

Making the dressing

See page 13.

> **Useful tip:** Handle the flesh of the pomelo with care. Bruising will give it a bitter taste.

Carrot and White Radish Salad
Gỏi cà rốt và củ cải trắng

White radish is well known for its strong flavour. In addition to its use in soup, it's widely incorporated in pickles and stock. Some people are put off by its strong flavour, but in a soup, it somehow becomes sweeter and earthier tasting. Moreover, white radish and carrot pickles are regularly used in Vietnamese dipping sauces, either to accompany dishes or to add to sandwiches. The pickles really uplift your appetite and add a slightly sour crunch.

In my opinion, this salad really showcases the flavour of white radish. Perhaps it's not to everyone's taste, but the whole point of trying new recipes is to experience new flavours, so I recommend giving it a try.

Ingredients (serves 6)

- 300g chicken breast
- Pinch of salt
- Pinch of ground black pepper
- ⅓ tsp Knorr seasoning
- 1 tsp oyster sauce
- 250ml white vinegar
- 150ml water
- 1 tsp sugar (with extra for sprinkling)
- 400g carrots
- 500g white radishes
- 250g onions
- 50g shallots
- Vegetable oil
- 50g mint (chopped)
- 50g coriander (chopped)
- 30g roasted peanuts

Marinating the chicken

1. Clean the chicken and leave in a colander until all the water has drained off it.
2. Butterfly the chicken using a sharp knife. Sprinkle with a little salt, black pepper, sugar, Knorr seasoning and oyster sauce. Leave to marinate for 20 minutes at room temperature.

Preparing the vegetables

1. In a small saucepan, mix the white vinegar, water and sugar. Bring to the boil and then set aside to cool.
2. Using a potato peeler or mandolin, thinly slice the carrots, white radishes and onions and place them in a bowl. Pour over the vinegar mixture, mix well and leave to marinate for 2 hours, stirring occasionally.

Frying the chicken

1. Heat a non-stick frying pan. When it's hot, drizzle in some oil and pan fry the chicken breast. Turn the heat down to medium. Turn the breast over when one side is golden.
2. When the meat is cooked through, remove from the heat and set aside. When the chicken has cooled down, cut into small pieces.

If you prefer, you can also grill the chicken. Simply turn the grill to a medium-high setting, drizzle a little oil on an oven tray and grill the chicken breasts until both sides are brown and the meat is cooked through.

Frying the shallots

Chop and sauté the shallots in 50ml of oil until lightly browned. Remove from the heat and keep stirring until they are evenly coloured. Set aside.

Putting the salad together

1. Take a clean tea towel, place the mixture of carrots, white radish and onion inside it and squeeze to remove all the liquid.
2. Place the vegetables on a large plate (5cm deep).
3. Arrange a layer of the chopped mint and coriander on the top.
4. Then add a layer of chicken breast, fried shallots and a sprinkling of roasted peanuts.
5. Finally, pour over the dressing and serve.

Making the dressing

See page 13.

> **Useful tip:** You can prepare each of the ingredients in advance and put them together just before serving.

Beef Noodle Soup
Phở Bò

Pho Bo is one of the most famous street foods in Vietnam, and it has come to be known globally. Every foreigner who comes to live in Vietnam knows about this dish, and they'll even tell you which street corner has the best Pho shop. It's a comfort food that gives you energy for most of the day.

Recipes for Pho vary according to location, as well as the individual cooking it. For me, simple and tasty is key. After years of experimenting and practising, I came up with this recipe. When my kids were small, they were very fussy about food. They didn't want to eat meat or anything they had to chew, so I added carrots to the soup so that at least there was something for them to eat. I realised that the vegetable added a natural sweetness to the dish. Cooking Pho is not difficult, you just need the right ingredients and technique.

Ingredients (serves 6-8)

- 1kg beef oxtail or beef bones
- 10g star anise
- 20g cinnamon sticks
- 2½ onions
- 100g ginger
- 2 carrots
- 2 tsp salt
- 3 chicken stock cubes
- 2 tbsp oyster sauce
- 2 tbsp fish sauce
- Vegetable oil
- 400g dry rice sticks
- 500g rump steak or, for luxury, use beef tenderloin
- 400g bean sprouts
- 2 limes
- 2 chillies
- Chilli sauce
- Hoisin sauce
- 200g spring onions (chopped)
- 100g coriander (chopped)

For the soup

1. Thoroughly clean the oxtail or bones with salt and rinse well with water. Add 4 litres of water to a large saucepan and bring to the boil. Add the oxtail. Remove any froth that appears on the surface of the water. Reduce the heat and leave to simmer, continuing to remove the froth until you have a clear soup.
2. Grill the star anise, cinnamon sticks and two of the onions in the oven until they are lightly burnt. Cut the ginger into strips and the carrots into large pieces. Put the ginger, star anise, cinnamon sticks and onions into a sheer bag and add them to the soup with the carrots.
3. Now add the salt, chicken stock cubes, oyster sauce and fish sauce. Finely chop the remaining onion half, sauté in 30ml of oil until golden brown and add to the soup. Leave to simmer for 3 to 4 hours under a lid. Then remove the oxtail and carrots.

Preparing the noodles and steak

1. Boil some water in a large saucepan. Add the rice sticks, reduce the heat and stir to separate. Cover with a lid, leaving a small gap.
2. Cook for 7 minutes, stir and taste. Pour the sticks into a large colander and drain them. Now rinse them thoroughly with cold water. Leave them to drain for a further hour before serving.
3. Clean the steak and drain the water from the meat using a colander. Use a sharp knife to remove all the fat and veins from the beef and thinly slice it.

Useful tip: When warming up the soup, never use a microwave. Add some water, bring it to the boil, reduce the heat and simmer for at least 1 hour before serving.

To serve

1. Blanch the bean sprouts in boiling water. Now drain them and put them in a dish. Cut up the limes and chillies and arrange them in small dishes. Serve the chilli and hoisin sauce in dishes, too, displaying all of them on the table.
2. Bring the soup to the boil. Taste and add seasoning if necessary. Put a small amount of the prepared rice sticks into individual bowls and warm them up in the microwave for 30 seconds. Sprinkle some spring onions and coriander over the top of them. Put a portion of the sliced beef into a ladle and dip it into the boiling soup for a few seconds. Add the cooked beef to the noodles and then cover with some of the soup. Continue until you have a bowl of soup for everyone around the table.
3. At the table, tell each guest to add to their soup a small amount of the bean sprouts, lime juice, chillies and chilli and hoisin sauces, to their taste.

Chicken Noodle Soup
Phở Gà

Chicken Noodle Soup is perhaps a slightly healthier version of Beef Noodle Soup. It's very popular in Vietnam, but somehow, it's not as famous internationally as its counterpart. When foreigners talk about Pho, they are generally referring to the beef variety. However, the distinctive taste of Chicken Noodle Soup is insanely good, so it would be such a shame for you to miss out on it.

Chicken is also a symbol of worship in Vietnam. If you have ever visited during the traditional New Year's holiday called Tet, you will see almost every household preparing a tray including chicken, fruit, a bowl of rice and some incense sticks. These are to thank the ancestors for the blessings we have been given.

Ingredients (seves 6-8)

- 1kg chicken bones (chicken carcass)
- 1 whole chicken (1-1.2kg)
- 10g star anise
- 20g cinnamon sticks
- 2½ onions
- 100g ginger
- 2 carrots
- 2 tsp salt
- 3 chicken stock cubes
- 2 tbsp oyster sauce
- 2 tbsp fish sauce
- Vegetable oil
- 400g rice sticks
- 400g bean sprouts
- 2 limes
- 2 chillies
- Chilli sauce
- Hoisin sauce
- 200g spring onions (chopped)
- 100g coriander (chopped)

Useful tip: To warm up the shredded chicken, place it in a sieve and steam it over the soup.

Preparing the soup

1. Clean the chicken bones and the chicken with salt and rinse them well with water. Add 4 litres of water to a large saucepan and bring to the boil. Add the chicken bones and the whole chicken. Remove any froth that appears on the surface of the water. Reduce the heat and leave to simmer, continuing to remove the froth until you have a clear soup.
2. Grill the star anise, cinnamon sticks and two of the onions in the oven until they are lightly burnt. Cut the ginger into strips and the carrots into large pieces. Put the ginger, star anise, cinnamon sticks and onions into a sheer bag and add them to the soup with the carrots.
3. Now add the salt, chicken stock cubes, oyster sauce and fish sauce. Finely chop the remaining onion half, sauté in 30ml of oil until golden brown and add to the soup. Simmer the soup for a further 30 minutes, then check the chicken.
4. When the chicken is cooked, remove it from the soup and leave it to cool. Then remove the meat from the bones and shred it. Simmer the soup for 1 hour under a lid. Afterwards, remove the remaining chicken bones and carrots then simmer for a further 2 hours.

Preparing the noodles

1. Boil some water in a large saucepan. Add the rice sticks, reduce the heat and stir to separate. Cover with a lid, leaving a small gap.
2. Cook for 7 minutes, stir and taste. Pour the sticks into a large colander and drain them. Now rinse them thoroughly with cold water. Leave them to drain for a further hour before serving.

To serve

1. Blanch the bean sprouts in boiling water. Now drain them and put them in a dish. Cut up the limes and chillies and arrange them in small dishes. Serve the chilli and hoisin sauces in dishes, too, displaying all of them on the table.
2. Bring the soup to the boil. Taste and add seasoning if necessary. Put a small amount of the prepared rice sticks into individual bowls and warm them up in the microwave for 30 seconds. Add some of the shredded chicken and sprinkle some spring onions and coriander over the top. Cover with some of the soup. Continue until you have a bowl of soup for everyone around the table.
3. At the table, tell each guest to add to their soup a small amount of the bean sprouts, lime juice, chillies and chilli and hoisin sauce, to their taste.

Sour Fish Soup
Canh chua cá

Vietnamese love to cook Sour Fish Soup, and it is served in most local restaurants in Vietnam, where it has a strong legacy. It's very simple, easy to make and refreshing, and it also goes well with the humid climate in Saigon. It's loaded with vegetables and fish, which are easy to digest, and it's also a great meal to eat when you are dieting. You can use any type of fish and, if you don't mind the bones (they add to the taste), you can even use the whole fish, as we often do.

The ingredients for this soup might not be attractive to everyone, however, it is one of the dishes from my childhood, and I personally love it.

Ingredients (serves 3)

- 300g white fish fillet or fish with bones
- 2 tomatoes
- 200g ripe pineapple (after removing skin and core)
- 150g okra
- 3 shallots (sliced)
- 1 garlic clove (crushed)
- 2 tbsp vegetable oil
- ⅓ tsp salt
- ½ chicken stock cube
- 1 tbsp oyster sauce
- ½ tbsp fish sauce
- 3 tbsp of tamarind juice (see page 9 for the recipe)
- A pinch of sugar
- 100g bean sprouts
- 1 chilli (chopped)
- 1 spring onion (chopped)
- Coriander, to use according to preference (chopped)

Preparing the vegetables

1. Clean the fish fillet, cut it into large chunks and set it aside. Cut the tomatoes and pineapple into small pieces. Cut the ends off the okra and cut it into small pieces too.
2. In a large saucepan over a high heat, fry the shallots and garlic in the oil. Add the tomatoes and pineapple, stir for 2 minutes, then add approximately 1 litre of water and bring to the boil. Add the salt, chicken stock, oyster sauce, fish sauce, tamarind juice and a pinch of sugar.
3. Bring to the boil once again. Add the fish fillet and cook for 5 minutes (10 if the fish has bones). Then add the okra and cook for a further 3 minutes before adding the bean sprouts.

To serve

1. After bringing the soup to the boil for one last time, remove it from the heat.
2. Serve garnished with the chopped chilli, spring onions and coriander.

Useful tip: When warming up the soup, never use a microwave. Add some water, bring it to the boil, reduce the heat and simmer for at least half an hour before serving.

Vietnamese Carrot and Cucumber Salad
Gỏi cà rốt và dưa leo

For most people, salad is one of the simplest, healthiest and easiest dishes to make. All you need are some green leaves and a bit of dressing and voila, it's ready.

But for Vietnamese folk, as well as being a healthy option, salad means enjoyment and indulgence. We only make this recipe for parties or gatherings or order it when we go to a restaurant. It requires a bit of work, but once you have tasted it you will want to eat it again and again. Carrots and cucumbers are the most basic vegetables for a Vietnamese salad because of their elastic texture. However, you can use any of your favourite vegetables (or ones that need using up), so long as they are flexible and don't break during the squeezing process.

Ingredients (serves 6)

- 250ml white vinegar
- 150ml water
- 1 tsp sugar
- 350g carrots
- 500g cucumbers
- 250g onions
- 50g mint (chopped)
- 50g coriander (optional, chopped)
- 50g shallots (sliced)
- 50ml vegetable oil
- 30g roasted peanuts

Preparing the vegetables

1. In a small saucepan, mix together the white vinegar, water and sugar. Bring to the boil and set aside to cool.
2. Using a potato peeler or mandolin, thinly slice the carrots, cucumbers and onions and put them in a bowl. Pour the vinegar mixture over them, mix well and then leave to marinate for 2 hours, stirring occasionally.

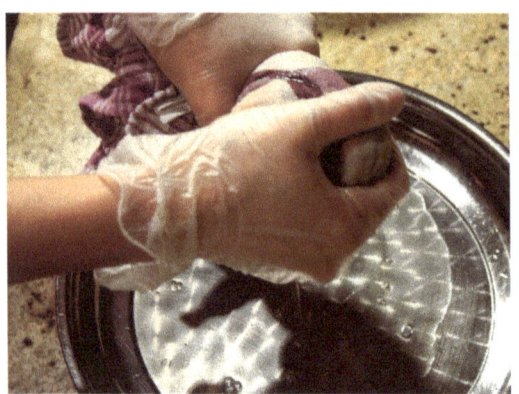

Squeezing process

1. Take a clean tea towel, place the mixture of carrots, cucumber and onion inside it and squeeze to remove all the liquid.
2. Place the vegetables on a large plate (circa 5cm deep). Sprinkle over the chopped mint and coriander.

Frying the shallots

1. Fry the sliced shallots in the oil until lightly browned and then remove from the heat.
2. Continue to stir until all the shallots are well coated with the oil. Set aside. When cool, pour them over the vegetables.

To serve

Sprinkle the crushed roasted nuts over the top of your vegetables and pour over the dressing.

Making the dressing

See page 13.

Fried Spring Rolls
Chả giò

Fried Spring Rolls have always been a key part of Vietnamese food culture, and they have played a major role in every gathering or party I have attended.

Depending on the region as well as the individual, the fillings used can vary. I favour the filling that is generally used in Saigon, because I was born and grew up in the South. My mum would put fresh crab meat in her rolls, which tasted absolutely sensational. She used to chop all the ingredients by hand, and it took her ages to prepare them.

I guess every country has its own version of savoury rolls, as they are an easy finger food and make good snacks. That also means they are a favourite addition to a party menu. Preparing Vietnamese Spring Rolls will take you a bit of time, but they are worth the effort. Instead of chopping all the ingredients by hand, you can always use a food processor.

Ingredients (serves 6)

- 20g dry wood ear mushrooms
- 500g medium tiger prawns
- 200g chicken breast
- 200g onion
- 150g fresh button mushrooms
- 300g taro (aravi)
- 40g glass noodles (cut into small strips of 2-3cm)
- 1 tsp ground black pepper
- Pinch of salt
- 30-40 pieces rice paper (15½cm)
- Vegetable oil
- 500g lettuce
- 200g mint
- 200g coriander

Preparing the ingredients

1. Soak the wood ear mushrooms overnight or for at least a few hours. Wash them thoroughly, discarding any hard bits.
2. Devein and fully clean the prawns before giving them a good rinse.
3. Wash the chicken breast, onion, button mushrooms and the taro (aravi) after removing the skin.
4. Soak the glass noodles in water for 5 minutes.
5. Leave all the ingredients to dry in a colander for at least 1 hour.

Making the filling

1. First, cut the chicken breast, onion and taro into large chunks and pop them in a blender to chop. Then add the prawns, button mushrooms and wood ear mushrooms and pulse to produce a fine (but not mushy) mixture.
2. Place the mixture in a large bowl, add the glass noodles, the ground black pepper and a pinch of salt, and mix thoroughly. This will be the filling for the spring rolls.

Rolling the rolls

1. Take 3 sheets of rice paper and moisten both sides with water.
2. Place them on a flat, non-absorbent surface. This will allow time for the first sheets to absorb the water, making them easier for you to roll.

Starting with the first sheet

1. With a tablespoon in each hand, use one spoon to scoop a small amount of filling, and the other to place it close to the edge nearest to you.
2. Fold it over, then fold in the sides and roll to complete the spring roll.
3. Repeat with the remaining sheets of rice paper.
4. Lightly brush a large tray with a thin layer of oil, so that the spring rolls don't stick to it.
5. Place the completed rolls in even rows on top, then leave them to dry (uncovered) for two hours before frying.

Frying the rolls

1. Fill a non-stick frying pan with oil to approximately a third of its depth.
2. When the oil is hot, gently put the spring rolls in the pan, leaving space between them to ensure they don't stick together.
3. Turn the heat down to medium or low, so that the spring rolls are thoroughly cooked through. If they do get stuck together, gently separate them with a knife. Discard any burnt bits from the oil.
4. Partly fry the rolls until they are cooked inside but not golden brown.
5. Remove them from the frying pan and put them in a sieve to drain any excess oil, then place them on a tray.
6. Leave them to cool down.
7. Just before serving, fry the spring rolls again until they are golden brown.

To serve

Set 2 plates on the table, one for the lettuce, mint and coriander, and another for the spring rolls. In addition, give each guest a small bowl filled with the dipping sauce.

Take a lettuce leaf and place some mint, coriander and a spring roll inside it. Fold it over and dip it in the sauce.

Making the dipping sauce

See page 12.

Useful tip: For the best results, prepare and partly fry the spring rolls in advance so that they are cooked through but not golden brown. Then store them in the fridge for up to three days. Fry them again just before serving.

Main Courses

Pan Fried Fish in Tomato Sauce
Cá chiên sốt cà

Stuffed Tofu in Tomato Sauce
Đậu hũ nhồi thịt xốt cà chua

La Vong Fish Cakes
Chả cá Lã Vọng

Chicken with Lemongrass and Chilli
Gà xào sả ớt

Stir Fried Mixed Vegetables with Beef
Rau thập cẩm xào với thịt bò

Tender Rolled Beef in Chinese Five Spice
Bò hầm cuốn Ngũ vị

Braised Fish
Cá kho

Southern Crispy Crepes
Bánh xèo Nam Bộ

Chicken with Ginger
Gà kho gừng

Stir Fried Beans with Prawns
Đậu que xào với Tôm

Prawns with Garlic and Chillies
Tôm rang với tỏi và ớt

Pan Fried Fish in Tomato Sauce
Cá chiên sốt cà

The humble tomato seems to play a major role in every country's cuisine. It can be used for just about everything, from preparing a simple salad to creating a restaurant-standard consommé. If you have a juicer at home, you can even make your own tomato juice. Just add a little bit of sugar and chill it in the fridge. I guarantee that it will be the freshest juice you have ever tasted.

In Vietnam, we use tomatoes in almost every meal to create a tangy taste and elevate the flavour. I learnt how to make this sauce from my mum. It's simple, quick and tastes great. The fantastic thing about it is that you can use it with any ingredients, including meats, tofu, vegetables and other seafood aside from fish. If you are sticking with fish, you can use any type you like.

Use the whole fish or cut it into small pieces, cooking it with or without the bones.

Ingredients (serves 4)

- 400g white fish fillets (any kind)
- Pinch of salt
- Pinch of ground black pepper
- 2 tomatoes
- 4 shallots
- 2 garlic cloves
- 2 red Thai chillies (optional)
- 3 tbsp vegetable oil
- 150ml water
- ¼ tsp sugar
- ⅓ chicken stock cube
- ½ tbsp oyster sauce
- ⅔ tbsp fish sauce
- 2 spring onions (garnish)
- A few coriander leaves (garnish)

Preparing the ingredients

1. Clean the fish fillets and drain the water using a colander.
2. Sprinkle a little salt and black pepper on both sides of the fish and leave it to marinate for 30 minutes.
3. Chop the tomatoes, shallots, garlic and chillies.

Frying the fish

1. Heat a frying pan and add 3 tablespoons of oil.
2. Fry the fish until both sides are golden brown. Remove and set aside.

Making the sauce

1. In the same frying pan, add a little more oil if required or take some out if there's too much.
2. Fry the shallots and garlic until golden brown. Add the chopped tomatoes, stir for 2 minutes, then add 150ml water to cover the tomatoes.
3. Bring to the boil and add the sugar, chillies, chicken stock and the oyster and fish sauces. Stir well and cook for 5 minutes.

Adding the fish

1. Add the fish to the sauce and then reduce the heat. Cover the pan with a lid and simmer for 30 minutes, gently turning the fish from time to time, until the juice has reduced to a sauce.
2. Season to taste.

To serve

1. Place the fish on a large, deep plate, pour the sauce over the top and garnish with the spring onions and coriander.
2. Serve with steamed jasmine rice.

Useful tip: Using a whole fish will enhance the flavour of the dish.

Stuffed Tofu in Tomato Sauce
Đậu hũ nhồi thịt xốt cà chua

I know tofu isn't to everyone's taste, and many people find it too plain, but it is extremely popular in South East Asia. As I grew up eating lots of different kinds of tasty tofu dishes, I could have easily become a vegetarian.

Vietnamese Buddhists have invented hundreds of distinctive vegetarian dishes made from tofu and vegetables that you can only find in my home country. The lunar month of July is the biggest fasting month for Buddhists in Vietnam. It's when we pay tribute and show our gratitude to our relatives that have passed away. We also do lots of charity work for the poor. Every temple opens its doors, and the monks and volunteers cook hundreds of delicious dishes made from tofu and vegetables. Everybody is welcome to eat for free.

While this dish is not vegetarian, I wanted to share it because I love the taste and I learned the recipe from my mum. Making it requires a pair of delicate hands and patience. It's like cooking therapy, as your mind must be completely relaxed. These days, you can't find it in any Vietnamese restaurants, and even Vietnamese families seem to have forgotten about it, but the dish has remained close to my heart.

Ingredients (serves 3)

- 10g dried wood ear mushrooms
- 200g medium tiger prawns
- 1 piece of Chinese firm tofu, 10cm × 10cm
- 100g chicken breast
- 6 shallots (chopped)
- Pinch of ground black pepper
- 300ml vegetable oil
- 2 tomatoes
- 1 garlic clove (crushed)
- 200ml water
- ¼ teaspoon salt
- ½ chicken stock cube
- ¼ teaspoon sugar
- ½ tablespoon oyster sauce
- ⅔ tablespoons fish sauce
- 2 red Thai chillies (optional)

Preparing the ingredients

1. Soak the wood ear mushrooms overnight and then wash them, discarding any hard bits.
2. Remove the heads and shells of the prawns and devein them. Give them a good rinse.
3. Rinse the fresh tofu in cold water and leave in a colander to drain.
4. Wash the chicken and put it in a separate colander with the prawns and mushrooms to drain.

Preparing the stuffing

1. Mince the chicken breast and prawns in a blender. Add the wood ear mushrooms so that they are chopped but not minced. Place the mixture in a bowl.
2. Add 3 chopped shallots, a pinch of salt and a pinch of black pepper. Mix thoroughly.

Inserting the stuffing

1. Cut the tofu into 6 large rectangular pieces. Gently pick up a piece and make an incision along the centre, but not too near the edge, otherwise it will break. (Don't worry if the tofu piece does break, as the stuffing will help to seal it.)
2. Using a teaspoon, place a small amount of stuffing evenly inside the tofu piece.
3. Continue until each tofu piece has been stuffed.

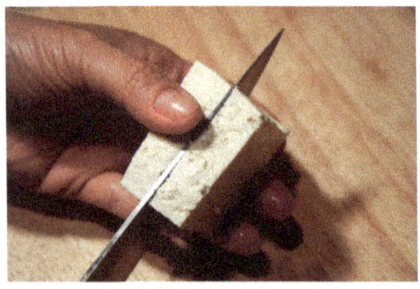

Frying the tofu

1. Heat approximately 300ml of oil in a medium-sized, non-stick frying pan and gently place the tofu in the oil. Turn the heat down to medium so it doesn't burn.
2. Fry the tofu pieces, rotating them until all the sides are golden brown. Remove from the pan.

Making the sauce

1. Roughly chop the tomatoes into small cubes. Using the same saucepan, remove the oil but keep about 2 tablespoons of it in the pan. Fry the 3 remaining chopped shallots with the crushed garlic until golden brown. Add the chopped tomatoes and cook for 5 minutes. Add the 200ml water, ¼ teaspoon salt, chicken stock cube, sugar, oyster sauce, fish sauce and chillies (if required).
2. Boil for 2 minutes, taste and then add the stuffed tofu. Put the lid on the pan and reduce the heat to medium.
3. Turning the tofu occasionally, simmer for 40 minutes until the juice has reduced to a sauce.
4. Serve with steamed jasmine rice.

> **Useful tip:** For the best texture, only use Chinese tofu for this dish. Japanese tofu is not suitable.

La Vong Fish Cakes
Chả cá Lã Vọng

Cha ca La Vong is a dish from a small area in Hanoi called Hang Son, which is often referred to as Cha Ca Town. During the French colonisation of Vietnam in the 1900s, the Doan family helped a group of soldiers called De Tham by letting them hide in their house away from French aggressors. The Doan family were known for their cooking skills, especially their fish cakes, and they made this dish many times to treat the soldiers during their secret stay.

Later, the De Tham soldiers opened a restaurant to show their appreciation to the family. A La Vong statue was placed inside it, which is a symbol of desiring a better life. This is where the name for the fish cakes was born.

Today, La Vong fish cakes hold legendary status. They are a real hidden gem because with just a few freely available ingredients, the dish has become a gastronomic delight. There are still some rustic Cha ca La Vong restaurants in Hanoi, where you are served at your table with a burnt charcoal stove and left to cook the dish yourself and enjoy it with shrimp paste. In this respect, I feel that it would be a waste not to share this fabulous dish with you. This is a recipe for when you want to gather everyone together, forget all your worries and cook and laugh.

Ingredients (serves 4)

- 1kg white fish fillet
- 300g galangal
- 30g shallots
- 4 garlic cloves
- 2 tsp turmeric powder
- ⅓ tsp salt
- ⅔ tbsp fish sauce
- ⅔ tbsp of oyster sauce
- ⅓ tsp ground black pepper
- A pinch of sugar
- 500g dry rice noodles
- 200g dill
- 300g spring onions
- Vegetable oil
- 100g roasted chopped peanuts

Marinating the fish

1. Wash the fish fillet and drain the excess water using a colander. Use an electric chopper to chop the galangal, shallots and garlic to a fine paste.
2. Cut the fish into cubes and put it in a bowl. Add the ground garlic, shallots and galangal. Then add the turmeric powder, salt, fish sauce, oyster sauce, black pepper and a pinch of sugar. Mix well and leave to marinate for 2 hours in the fridge.

Preparing the noodles

1. Fill a large saucepan with water and bring to the boil. Add the rice noodles, reduce the heat and stir to separate them.
2. Put the lid on the saucepan but leave a small gap and cook the noodles for 20 minutes. Stir and taste.
3. When cooked, pour the noodles into a large colander and rinse them thoroughly with cold water. Leave to drain for 1 hour before serving.

Preparing the vegetables

1. Cut the dill and 200g of the spring onions into strips about 3-4cm long. Place them on a plate.
2. Finely chop the remaining spring onions and fry them in 2 tablespoons of oil for 1 minute. Remove from the heat.

Frying the fish

1. Heat a non-stick frying pan and add approximately 200ml of oil. Arrange a layer of fish cubes evenly in the pan and fry them on each side until lightly browned.
2. When the fish cubes are cooked, remove them from the pan and set aside. Repeat with the remaining cubes until all of them are cooked.

Setting the table

On a table, arrange a plate of noodles, a plate of fried fish, a plate of dill and spring onions, a bowl of fried spring onions, a bowl of roasted nuts, a bowl of sweetened fish sauce and a small jug of oil. (You will also need a portable gas stove and a small frying pan.)

Making the sweetened fish sauce

See page 13.

To serve

Turn on the gas stove and heat the frying pan. When it's hot, drizzle in some oil. Add a small amount of the dill and spring onions, stir quickly and then add some fish. Stir again and serve on a small plate.

Putting the dish together

Each guest is invited to place some noodles, fried spring onions, roasted nuts, sweetened fish sauce and the fried fish with dill and spring onion in their bowl. They can then mix it all together before eating.

Useful tip: The idea of this dish is to gather friends and family together. Everyone then takes it in turns to cook the fish at the table.

Chicken with Lemongrass and Chilli
Gà xào sả ớt

This recipe is an everyday meal in Vietnam. Families normally sit together and share out dishes between them. There are often three on offer: a plate of meat or fish, a vegetable stir fry and a bowl of soup. I have always loved this dish as part of the trio.

Many different types of chicken are available, but we prefer free-range, which are raised in the Vietnamese countryside. You can easily tell the difference between free-range and factory chicken. The former is generally skinnier, the skin is a bright yellow, sunny colour and the meat tastes sweeter. We use all parts of the chicken, as cooking meat with the bones attached makes the dish much more flavourful.

I can still remember watching my mum using a cleaver to chop the lemongrass, chillies, shallots and garlic, which she did until they were minced almost to a paste.

This simple homemade dish is extremely easy to make and tastes delicious. Luckily, there are now tools available to help you with the chopping, and you can use any part of the chicken you like. I enjoy the bony bits while my husband prefers breast meat. My recipe has a bit of a twist to give the dish a bit more flare.

Ingredients (serves 3)

- 3 lemongrass sticks
- 2 red Thai chillies
- 5 shallots
- 2 garlic cloves
- 500g chicken breast (or any other parts)
- ⅓ tsp salt
- ⅓ tsp ground black pepper
- ½ tsp Knorr seasoning
- 1 tsp turmeric powder
- 1½ tsp ground Chinese five spice
- 2 tbsp of vegetable oil
- 150ml coconut juice
- 50ml water
- ½ chicken stock cube
- ⅔ tbsp fish sauce
- ⅔ tbsp oyster sauce

Chopping the vegetables

1. Take the lemongrass sticks and remove the dry root ends and the dry outer leaf, retaining only the thick part of the herb. Chop each stick into 0.5cm long pieces.
2. In a blender, grind the lemongrass, chillies, shallots and garlic to a fine paste.

Marinating the chicken

1. Wash the chicken, drain the excess water from the meat, cut it into large cubes and place it in a bowl.
2. Add the ground lemongrass mixture, salt, ground black pepper, Knorr seasoning, turmeric powder and ground Chinese five spice. Mix well and leave to marinate for 1 hour.

Cooking the chicken

1. In a non-stick saucepan, heat 2 tablespoons of oil over a high heat.
2. Place the marinated chicken in the pan and stir fry until it is lightly browned. Add the coconut juice and 50ml of water. Bring to the boil, removing any froth that appears on the surface.

Adding sauce

1. To the saucepan, add the chicken stock cube, fish sauce and oyster sauce. Stir. Leave for 3 minutes over a high heat and stir again.
2. Turn the heat down, put the lid on the saucepan and leave to cook for 45 minutes, adding some water if necessary. Stir occasionally until the water has reduced to a sauce.
3. Serve with steamed jasmine rice.

Useful tip: When chopping the lemongrass before putting it in the blender, don't cut it too long, as this will give a stringy texture to the dish.

Stir Fried Mixed Vegetables with Beef
Rau thập cẩm xào với thịt bò

Although you can use any vegetables you like for a stir fry, when I do one, I like to use the ones that really complement each other. I like the sweet taste of the carrots, the crunch of the beans and baby corn and the pleasantly bitter taste of the pak choi. Furthermore, the colour combination makes the dish burst with vibrancy.

After testing and lots of practice, I would like to share my experience of cooking a delicious stir fry. Each step is there for a reason, so don't rush anything. You want to be able to feel the texture of each element while enjoying the taste of the individual flavours.

Ingredients (serves 4)

- 300g rump steak (or any cuts available)
- Pinch of ground black pepper
- ½ tsp Knorr seasoning
- 3 garlic cloves (crushed)
- 2 carrots
- 200g Kenyan green beans
- 100g baby corn
- 200g pak choi
- Vegetable oil
- 50ml of water
- ¼ tsp salt
- ½ chicken stock cube
- ⅔ tablespoon fish sauce
- 1 tbsp oyster sauce

Marinating the beef

1. Rinse the beef under the tap, then drain the water from the meat using a colander.
2. Use a sharp knife to remove all the fat and veins from the beef and thinly slice it.
3. Add a pinch of salt and ground black pepper and the Knorr seasoning and crushed garlic.
4. Mix well and leave to marinate for 30 minutes in the fridge.

Preparing the vegetables

1. Remove the skin and the ends of the carrots, then cut them into 3-4cm long strips. Remove the ends of the beans and cut them in half. Cut the baby corn in half. Wash all the vegetables well and drain the excess water using a colander.
2. Remove the roots of the pak choi and cut along the length of the leaves. Wash and drain them in a separate colander.

Frying the beef

1. Heat a frying pan over a high heat. Drizzle in 2 tablespoons of oil and then add the beef.
2. Stir fry quickly for 3-5 minutes, until the meat is golden brown. Remove from the pan and set aside.

Stir frying the vegetables

1. Still using a high heat, drizzle 3 tablespoons of oil into the same frying pan and add the carrots, beans and baby corn.
2. Stir well, adding 50ml of water, ¼ teaspoon salt, the chicken stock and the fish and oyster sauces. Mix well and leave to cook for 4 minutes.

Putting everything together

When the water has reduced, add the pak choi and mix well, cooking for a further minute. Add the beef and mix again. Taste the pak choi to make sure it is cooked but still has a crunch, then remove from the heat and serve the stir fry with steamed jasmine rice.

Useful tip: You can use other cuts of beef, but in my experience, rump steak is the best for a stir fry.

Tender Rolled Beef in Chinese Five Spice
Bò hầm cuốn Ngũ vị

My mum cooked this dish for my husband back when we were dating. According to her, because he is English, he would love meat – and she was right.

This dish is a celebration of east meets west. It's meaty and full of Asian flavours. In Vietnam, we tend to view beef dishes as quite heavy, with strong tasting sauces, but this one is surprisingly light. The beef is the most tender I have tasted; when you bite into it, it just melts in your mouth. The natural sweetness of the carrots and coconut juice is taken on by the meat and is coupled with the distinctive flavour of the Chinese five spice.

I often cook this dish when we have a dinner party, and all my friends love it.

Ingredients (serves 4)

- 1.2kg ribeye (or any cuts containing fat)
- ⅓ tsp salt
- 5 garlic cloves (crushed)
- 3 tsp Chinese five spice
- 1 tsp Knorr seasoning
- ⅓ tsp ground black pepper
- 2 carrots
- 200g spring onions
- 1 small onion
- Vegetable oil
- 200ml coconut juice
- 100ml water
- ½ chicken stock cube
- ⅔ tbsp fish sauce
- 1 tbsp oyster sauce

Seasoning the beef

1. If the beef contains a lot of fat, trim some but not all of it, as this will ensure the meat stays moist. Cut it into large, 1cm thick pieces and use a meat tenderiser to make it thinner.
2. Mix the beef with the salt, garlic, Chinese five spice, Knorr seasoning and ground black pepper. Leave to marinate for 1 hour in the fridge.

Preparing the vegetables

1. Peel the carrots and cut them into 4-5cm long strips.
2. Separate the leaves of the spring onions and soak them in boiling water for 1 minute. Leave to drain.

Rolling the beef

1. Place a piece of beef on a flat surface, put 4-5 pieces of carrot in the middle of it and roll it.
2. Take a piece of spring onion leaf and use it to tie around the beef roll. Repeat with the next slice of beef.

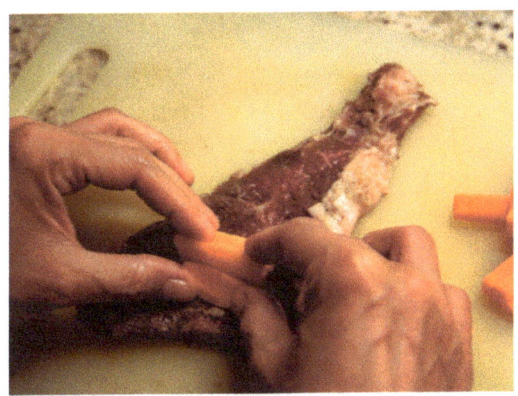

Cooking the beef

1. Slice the onion into small wedges. Using a deep, non-stick frying pan or a large saucepan, heat 2 tablespoons of oil and add the onion. Stir and add the beef rolls in an even layer. When one side of the roll is cooked, turn it over.
2. When the meat juice has reduced, add the coconut juice and 100ml of water. Stir gently, close the lid and bring to the boil, removing any froth that appears on the surface.

Adding the seasoning

1. When the sauce is clear, add the chicken stock cube and the fish and oyster sauces. Turn the heat to medium, put the lid on the pan and leave to simmer for 1 hour, adding some water if necessary.
2. Turn the rolls over occasionally until the water has reduced to a sauce and the meat is tender. Serve with steamed jasmine rice.

> **Useful tip:** When warming up the beef rolls, always heat them on the stove and not in the microwave. Add a little water to the rolls, and when it starts to boil, reduce the heat and simmer for at least 30 minutes, turning the rolls over so they are heated throughout.

Braised Fish
Cá kho

Braised Fish is a traditional folk dish from the Vietnamese countryside. Back in the olden days, many Vietnamese people were farmers, as they still are. Their dishes were created from the catch of the day and homegrown vegetables from their back gardens. After a hard day working in the fields, they might go fishing on the way home and then prepare a quick meal with grilled or fried fish paired with a rustic soup and some stir fried or boiled vegetables.

Braised Fish was also popular. Our ancestors would put all the ingredients in a clay pot, before cooking their dish over a bed of straw. This recipe is popular throughout Vietnam, though the ingredients may vary depending on the area in which it's made. My mum taught me how to cook this particular dish. The vegetables she put in it might sound strange to you, but the combination really works and tastes delicious. You can use any kind of fish you like and cook either the fillets or the whole fish, including the bones.

Ingredients (serves 3)

- 500g fish fillet or fish with bones
- 200g ripe pineapple (after removing skin and core)
- 2 tomatoes
- 2 garlic cloves (crushed)
- 5 shallots (chopped)
- 2 small red Thai chillies (chopped)
- ½ tsp salt
- Pinch of sugar
- ⅓ tsp ground black pepper
- 1-2 tbsp vegetable oil
- 50ml water
- 100ml coconut juice
- ½ chicken stock cube
- 1 tbsp oyster sauce
- ⅔ tbsp fish sauce
- 1 tbsp blackened caramelised sauce (see page 14 for the recipe)

Preparing the fish pot

1. Wash the fish fillet and drain the water from it using a colander. Once dry, cut it into large chunks.
2. Cut the pineapple and tomatoes into small pieces.
3. Arrange a layer of pineapple and tomatoes over the bottom of a non-stick saucepan. Top with a layer of fish, continuing with alternate layers. (I recommend 2 layers each.)

Seasoning the dish

1. When you have finished the layers, add the crushed garlic, chopped shallots, chillies, salt, sugar and ground black pepper.
2. Drizzle 1-2 tablespoons of oil over the top.

Cooking the pot

1. Over a high heat, bring the fish pot to the boil and leave it to cook for 5 minutes until the liquor has reduced.
2. Add 50ml water and the coconut juice and bring to the boil, removing any froth that appears on the surface of the stock.

Adding the seasoning

1. To the pot, add the chicken stock, the oyster and fish sauces and the blackened caramelised sauce. Stir gently.
2. Turn the heat down to low, put the lid on the pot and leave to simmer for 60 minutes. Check occasionally, adding some extra water if necessary.

To serve

When the stock has reduced, remove from the heat and serve with steamed jasmine rice.

> **Useful tips:** Don't stir the pot too much or you will break the delicate texture of the fish. Always make sure there is liquid in the dish to prevent it from burning.

Southern Crispy Crepes
Bánh xèo Nam Bộ

Even in the height of summer, the residents of Saigon, if not all of Vietnam, like to eat hot and spicy food. Quite often in a tiny corner of the local market, you'll find a crowd of people squeezing between all the rusty stools and tables to enjoy bowls of food swimming with chillies.

Whenever I'm back home, I often go to the market and sit on one of those stools, where one of my favourite dishes is Southern Crepes. I love sitting there and watching the lady pour a ladle of 'liquid flour' into a frying pan. The sound of the wet flour sizzling in hot oil heated over the red-hot embers of a charcoal stove makes me feel happy.

Ingredients (serves 6)

- 800g medium tiger prawns
- 300g chicken breast
- 400g bean sprouts
- 250g onions
- 300g rice flour (Thai made)
- 100g tapioca flour
- ¾ tsp baking powder
- 400ml coconut milk
- 500ml water
- 1 tsp turmeric powder
- Pinch of salt
- 3 tbsp chopped spring onion
- Vegetable oil
- 500g lettuce
- 200g mint
- 200g coriander

Preparing the stuffing

1. Fully clean the prawns, chicken breast and bean sprouts, and drain the water using a colander.
2. Cut the prawns into small pieces and thinly slice the chicken and onions.

Preparing the pancake mix

1. In a large bowl, mix the rice flour, tapioca flour and baking powder with the coconut milk, 500ml water, turmeric powder, a pinch of salt and the spring onions.
2. Mix thoroughly, ensuring there are no lumps. Set aside for 30 minutes.

For the filling

1. Put a flat, non-stick frying pan (21cm) over a high heat. Drizzle some oil into the pan and add some onion, chicken and prawns.
2. Stir and put the lid on the pan for 1 minute.

Pouring the flour mixture

1. Arrange the filling in an even layer around the pan.
2. Stir the crepe flour mixture before taking a full ladle (50ml) and pouring it into the pan in a thin layer.
3. To complete the round, take another half ladle of the flour mixture and pour it into the gap.
4. Turn the pan around to make sure the mixture spreads evenly and thinly. Cover the pan with a lid. Reduce the heat to medium-low and cook for 8 minutes, checking it occasionally by using a spatula to lift the edge of the crepe.

Useful tip: As these crepes take time to prepare, you can cook them in advance and warm them up in the oven at 200°C before serving, turning gently over so both sides are cooked.

Cooking the crepe

1. When lifting the lid, remember not to turn it to the side because the condensation will drip into the pan and make the oil splash. Instead, put it straight onto a plate next to it.
2. Lift the edge of the crepe to check it. When it is golden brown, put a small amount of the bean sprouts over one half of the crepe. Put the lid back on and cook for 30 seconds. Carefully lift one end up, fold it in half and place it on a large plate.
3. Repeat to make the rest of the crepes.

To serve/eat

1. Take a lettuce leaf and sprinkle inside it a few mint and coriander leaves. Now add a small piece of the crepe and filling.
2. Fold the lettuce leaf over and dip it into the dipping fish sauce.

Making the dipping fish sauce

See page 12.

Chicken with Ginger
Gà kho gừng

This is one of my favourite homemade dishes. I know lots of people don't like ginger, and I personally don't like it when it's raw, as it can overpower the other ingredients and its strong taste can overwhelm your palate. However, after it's been cooked with other ingredients, it becomes tender and sweet and has a slightly spicy taste. I often find myself preferring the ginger to the chicken, but that's just me!

You can use any parts of the chicken you like. I personally favour cooking chicken with the bones, as it gives a deeper flavour to the dish. This recipe is the ultimate homemade comfort food, and it can make a great main dish for a dinner party.

Ingredients (serves 3)

- 500g chicken breast (or any other parts)
- 150g ginger
- ⅓ tsp salt
- ⅓ tsp ground black pepper
- 1 tsp Knorr seasoning
- 2 tsp vegetable oil
- 100ml water
- 100ml coconut juice
- ½ chicken stock cube
- ⅔ tbsp fish sauce
- ⅔ tbsp oyster sauce
- ⅔ tbsp blackened caramelised sauce (see page 14 for recipe)

Marinating the chicken

1. Wash the chicken and use a colander to shake off the excess water.
2. Cut the chicken into large cubes. Peel the ginger and cut it into strips.
3. Place the chicken in a bowl and add the salt, ground black pepper, ginger and Knorr seasoning. Leave to marinate for around 1 hour.

Cooking the chicken

1. Heat the oil in a saucepan, add the marinated chicken and cook for a few minutes, stirring occasionally. Add the water and coconut juice. Bring to the boil, removing any froth that appears on the surface.
2. Add the chicken stock cube, fish sauce, oyster sauce and blackened caramelised sauce and mix well. Reduce the heat.

Simmering

1. Put the lid on the saucepan. Turn the heat down to medium. Leave to simmer for about 45 minutes, stirring occasionally until the water reduces to a sauce. (If it's looking a little dry during this process, add some more water.)
2. Serve with steamed jasmine rice.

Useful tip: For a clear sauce, always remove the froth.

Stir Fried Beans with Prawns
Đậu que xào với Tôm

Vietnamese people stir fry something practically every day. It's quick, easy and healthy, as you use very little oil and generally include a variety of vegetables. Some people carefully select ingredients that complement each other, whilst others take what's available in the fridge and toss it all together in a wok or frying pan.

Over the years, I have tasted many different stir fries from a variety of countries, however, I still think my mum's recipe is the best. The smell of the garlic frying is intoxicating, and all my friends and family love the dish. We are living in an age when there are unlimited supplies of amazing local produce, so we should make the most of them.

Ingredients (serves 4)

- 500g medium tiger prawns
- 400g Kenyan fine beans
- Ground black pepper
- ½ tsp Knorr seasoning
- 4 tbsp vegetable oil
- 3 garlic cloves (finely chopped)
- 100ml water
- ¼ tsp salt (with extra for sprinkling)
- ⅔ tbsp fish sauce
- 1 tbsp oyster sauce
- ½ chicken stock cube

Preparing the prawns and beans

1. Fully clean the prawns and remove the heads and shells. Devein and rinse well. Leave to drain in a colander.
2. Cut the ends off the beans and slice them in half. Rinse well and leave to drain.
3. Place the prawns in a bowl and sprinkle them with a pinch of salt, ground black pepper and Knorr seasoning. Leave them to marinate for 30 minutes.

Frying the prawns

1. On a high heat, drizzle 2 tablespoons of oil in a frying pan, add the garlic and stir quickly.
2. Add the prawns. Stir for 3 minutes until the garlic is golden brown and the prawns are cooked. Remove and set aside.

Frying the beans

1. To the same frying pan, add 2 tablespoons of oil and the beans. Stir for 2 minutes before adding 100ml of water. Now add the ¼ teaspoon of salt, fish sauce, oyster sauce and chicken stock cube.
2. Stir well and leave to cook for 4 minutes.

Adding the prawns

1. Stir again and taste the beans to make sure they are cooked.
2. When the water has reduced, add the cooked prawns. Mix well, making sure that the prawns are heated through. Remove from the heat and serve with steamed jasmine rice.

Useful tip: To maintain a firm texture, ensure all the water has drained from the prawns before marinating and frying them.

Prawns with Garlic and Chillies
Tôm rang với tỏi và ớt

We are lucky to currently live in the heart of the Gulf region, where there is an endless supply of fresh seafood, and we are spoilt for choice. When we arrived, I was inspired to create a new dish with just some basic ingredients.

When it comes to seafood, we tend to use minimal marinating so the main ingredient can 'sing for itself'. For example, we often just marinate prawns with a bit of salt and black pepper before grilling, boiling or deep frying them. I have done so much of this kind of cooking that I was keen to try something else. I wanted my prawns to sing for themselves while at the same time harmonising with the other ingredients.

Prawns with Garlic and Chillies is such a simple dish and requires minimal effort. To make things even simpler, you can even ask your fishmonger to help you with the cleaning process.

Ingredients (serves 4)

- 8 jumbo tiger prawns or large tiger prawns
- 3 garlic cloves
- 2 small red Thai chillies
- ⅓ tsp salt
- 1 tsp Knorr seasoning
- ¼ tsp sugar
- ¼ tsp ground black pepper
- 2 tbsp vegetable oil
- 50ml water
- ⅓ chicken stock cube
- 1 tbsp oyster sauce
- ⅔ tbsp fish sauce

Preparing and marinating the prawns

1. Remove the heads, guts and devein but retain the shell and rinse well. Leave to drain in a colander.
2. Slice the garlic and chillies and put them in a large bowl with the prawns, salt, Knorr seasoning, sugar and ground black pepper. Mix well and leave to marinate for 30 minutes in the fridge.

Frying the prawns

1. Heat a frying pan over a high heat and add 2 tablespoons of oil followed by the prawns.
2. Partially cook the prawns, turning them over until they are pink.
3. Add 50ml of water, the chicken stock and the oyster and fish sauces. Give everything a stir.

Serving the prawns

1. Leave the prawns to cook for about 5 minutes, turning them over again until the liquor reduces.
2. Remove from the heat and serve with steamed jasmine rice.

> **Useful tip:** Cooking the prawns with the shells on will keep them moist and improve their sweetness.

Desserts

Banana Fritters With Ice Cream
Chuối chiên với kem

Banana Cake
Bánh Chuối nướng

Pineapple Tartlets
Bánh Tạc nhân thơm

Tapioca Cake
Bánh khoai mì

Banana Fritters With Ice Cream
Chuối chiên với kem

Banana fritters with ice cream tops the list for many people as their favourite dessert. Just imagine biting into hot, crispy, battered banana combined with cold vanilla ice cream. You just want to close your eyes and enjoy the hot and cold sensations lingering in your mouth.

This dish was one of my childhood treats, and it still is. I can recall going to my local market in Saigon, where I often spotted a lady sitting in a corner with two large baskets beside her. In one of them was a large frying pan filled with seriously hot oil, and she would be skilfully frying one battered banana after another. I couldn't resist the sunny, golden-brown colour of the fruit and the sweet, tempting smell. I just had to stop and get one.

There are so many recipes for making the batter. Lots of people like to use breadcrumbs to make the bananas really crispy, but I find they tend to absorb too much oil. Alternatively, my recipe achieves a light and crispy result.

Ingredients (serves 5-6)

- 300g all-purpose flour
- 150g Thai rice flour
- ¾ tsp yeast
- 600ml cool water
- 800g ripe bananas (any kind)
- Vegetable oil

Making the batter

1. Mix together the all-purpose flour, Thai rice flour and yeast.
2. Slowly pour approximately 600ml of cool water into the mixture and stir thoroughly. Make sure there are no lumps, and the consistency is thick enough to coat the bananas well. Set aside for 30 minutes.

Alternative – Thai tempura flour

As a shortcut, you can just use Thai tempura flour. Slowly pour 350ml of cool water into 300g of flour. Mix and stir thoroughly, ensuring there are no lumps, and that the consistency of the mixture is slightly thick in order to coat the bananas well. Set aside for 30 minutes.

Preparing the bananas

1. If the bananas are on the large side, cut them in half, using your knife to flatten them down a little.
2. Stir the batter thoroughly before gently dropping the bananas into it and coating them well.

Frying the bananas

1. Heat enough oil to cover half the depth of a medium, non-stick saucepan.
2. When the oil is hot, use a fork to gently drop the coated bananas into it. Deep fry them, turning the heat down a little.
3. When one side of the banana is golden yellow, turn it over. Drain the oil from the cooked bananas using a sieve and serve them with vanilla ice cream.

Useful tip: Don't use a kitchen towel to try to remove oil from the bananas, as it will stick.

Banana Cake
Bánh Chuối nướng

Growing up after the war, life was really tough. We lived on charity goods from other countries. I still remember queuing up at 6 am every day to get bread, flour and old rice, or whatever our local authority provided that day. Occasionally, my mum used the bread to make a banana cake, which she baked in a large saucepan after arranging burnt charcoal around it.

As I got older, I forgot all about the flavour of the cake. After marrying my husband, we often found ourselves throwing away stale bread or else leaving it out for the birds. My husband also liked to eat bananas, but he left some of them until they were so ripe they were inedible, and I had to throw them away. Then I found a recipe for a cake that made the best use of old bread and ripe bananas. When I baked it for the first time, the smell wafting through the house was so sensational that I knew we were in for a real treat. In my opinion, a slice of banana caked paired with a scoop of vanilla ice cream is pure perfection!

Ingredients (serves 6-8)

- 800g ripe bananas
- 200g sugar
- 400ml coconut milk
- 2 drops of vanilla extract
- 70g melted butter
- 1 small loaf of bread

Preparing the bananas

1. Slice the bananas diagonally and place them in even rows on a large tray.
2. Sprinkle some sugar over the top of them, ensuring all the bananas are covered. Leave until the sugar has dissolved.

Cooking the coconut milk

1. Over a low heat, cook the remaining sugar in the coconut milk, stirring until the sugar has dissolved.
2. Add the vanilla extract and leave to cool.

Arranging the bananas

1. Coat a glass baking dish (23cm diameter/6cm deep) with melted butter.
2. Remove any undissolved sugar from the surface of the sliced banana.
3. Arrange a layer of banana in the dish.

Arranging the bread

1. Remove the crusts from the bread and soak the slices in the sweetened coconut milk before laying them on top of the banana.
2. Add another layer of banana and another layer of bread. Finally, finish with the rest of the banana slices.

Baking the cake

1. Drizzle the remaining butter over the top of the cake. Cover with foil and bake in the oven at 160°C for approximately 1hr 45 minutes, or until it is golden brown all over.
2. Ensure the cake is cooked through by inserting a serving knife into the centre. If it's clean when you remove it, the cake is good to go. Leave it to rest for a few hours before removing it from the dish and serving it with vanilla ice cream if desired.

Useful tip: When arranging the layers of sliced banana, ensure you remove all the undissolved sugar. This will stop the cake tasting of burnt sugar.

Pineapple Tartlets
Bánh Tạc nhân thơm

I have always been fond of these cute little tartlets, and after trying and failing to find a recipe for them, I came up with this wonderful, mouth-watering method. The result is delicious, especially when you eat your tartlet when it's still a bit warm. The soft but crunchy sweet dough combines wonderfully with the slightly tangy pineapple jam. And it's fabulous paired with a cup of tea.

My daughter is a big fan of these tartlets, and she can eat one after another. They make a great small treat for kids' lunchboxes. You can even make them with your children and get them involved in making and rolling the dough.

Ingredients (serves 6-8)

Filling
- 500g ripe, finely chopped pineapple (after removing the skin and core)
- 150g white sugar
- 2 drops vanilla extract

Dough
- 500g plain flour
- 250ml milk
- 250g soft butter
- 100g sugar
- 1 egg (beaten)

For the pineapple

1. You can often get pineapple that has already been cut into pieces. If you buy an uncut one, cut the ends off before slicing off the skin. As you can see from the pictures, the black eyes will lie diagonally. To remove them make 'V' shaped cuts starting at the top of the pineapple. Now turn the pineapple around in your hand and cut following the line of black eyes to the bottom. Do the same with the next line.
2. Cut the pineapple into 4 pieces and remove the core.

For the filling

1. Mix the chopped pineapple with the sugar. Over a high heat, dissolve the sugar, give it a stir and then turn the heat down to medium. Simmer the mixture, stirring occasionally.
2. When the mixture begins to thicken, add the vanilla extract, turn the heat to low and stir continuously until there is no liquid (while being careful not to let it burn).
3. Remove from the heat, stir and leave to cool.

For the dough

Except for the egg, blend all the ingredients for the dough in a food processor until smooth.

Rolling the dough

1. Lightly flour your work surface and knead the dough for 5 minutes to ensure a smooth texture.
2. Using a rolling pin, roll the dough to a thickness of about 3mm.

Cutting the shapes

1. To make the tartlet bases, use a round pastry cutter (7.5cm).
2. Cut the remaining dough into small strips.
3. Place the bases in an appropriate, non-stick baking tray. Scoop a full teaspoon of the pineapple mixture to fill each base.
4. Lay the dough strips in a crisscross pattern over the top.
5. Tidy up around the edges. Brush each tartlet with the egg and bake them in the oven at 150°C for approximately 1 hour until golden brown.

> **Useful tip:** To avoid soggy tartlets, make sure there is no liquid in the pineapple filling.

125

Tapioca Cake
Bánh khoai mì

Tapioca Cake is made from cassava roots, and it is one of my favourite desserts (but also a nice snack). When you look at the roots, you cannot believe that these ugly, rough looking things could produce such an amazing cake. Of course, there is work involved in making it, too, but that's another story.

I can still remember as a child helping my mum by grating the roots by hand. It took me ages to do, and afterwards, my back, arms and hands would be aching like mad. Just imagine sitting on a basic wooden stool, in one position, and grating a few kilos of roots for at least an hour… I certainly couldn't do it now!

Lucky for us, there are electric blenders available now, with different blades that can help with the once arduous grating process, as I'll go on to show you. It'll save you a lot of time, as this recipe requires a bit of attention. One of the great things about this cake is that it's egg free, so it's suitable for people who wouldn't normally be able to touch this kind of dessert. You will have to be a bit patient when making it, as there are a few steps involved, but once it's done, you'll see that all your hard work was worth it… I promise!

Ingredients (serves 6-8)

- 2kg tapioca roots (cassava roots)
- 200ml condensed milk
- 200g sugar
- 400ml coconut milk
- 70g melted butter

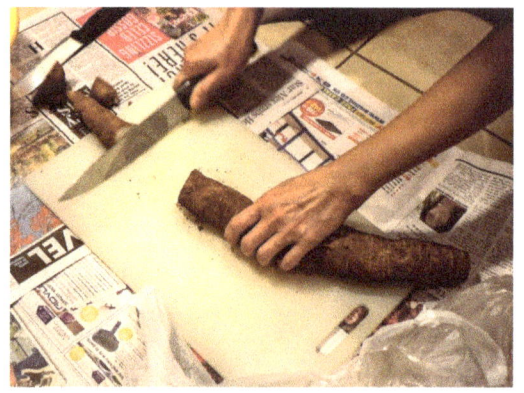

Removing the skin of the tapioca roots

1. Cut off the ends of the root. If it is too long, cut it in half and then cut deep, long lines along the body.
2. Use a sharp knife to lift the skin and then peel it off to reveal the white flesh inside.
3. Cut the root in half again and then cut each half into quarters along the length. Remove the fibre in the middle.

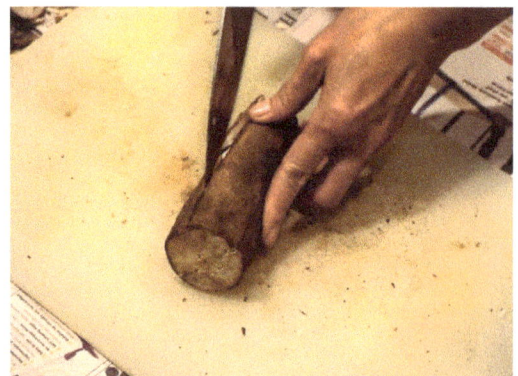

Cleaning the roots

1. Be sure to remove any parts that smell or appear off.
2. Wash the roots thoroughly and cut into large chunks. Soak in salt water for 15 minutes.
3. Rinse and then soak in fresh water for a further hour.

Grating the roots

1. Grate the tapioca pieces, using a hand grater or a food processor with a fine grating disk.
2. Change to the cutting blade, add all the bits that aren't grated and chop them up. For a smooth cake, ensure the tapioca is minced thoroughly, with no lumps.

Squeezing the minced tapioca

1. Soak the grated tapioca in fresh water for 30 minutes.
2. Place small amounts of it inside a clean tea towel and squeeze to remove the excess water.
3. Put the semi-dry tapioca in a bowl and repeat the process until all your tapioca has been squeezed.

Measuring the ingredients

1. Now measure the ingredients again. Mix every 500g of tapioca thoroughly with 200ml of condensed milk, 200g of sugar and 400ml of coconut milk.
2. Stir well until there are no lumps in the mixture.

Baking

1. Coat a glass dish (22.5cm diameter/6cm deep) with melted butter and pour the mixture to a depth of 3.5cm.
2. Drizzle the remaining butter over the top of the mixture and cover the dish with foil.
3. Bake in the oven at 150°C for approximately 2 hours or until it is golden brown all over. Remove from the mould after a few hours and serve.

> **Useful tip:** By using a glass dish, you can check all parts of the cake. Turn the dish around occasionally to ensure it is being cooked evenly.

www.ingramcontent.com/pod-product-compliance
Lightning Source LLC
Chambersburg PA
CBHW042025100526
44587CB00029B/4305